The Usborne
Famous Composers
Picture Book

Anthony Marks

Illustrated by Galia Bernstein
Designed by Jamie Ball

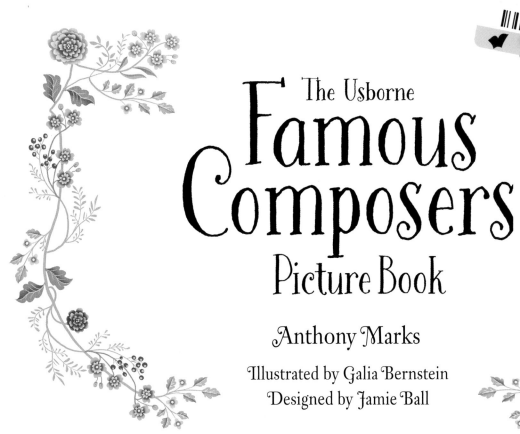

Contents

The First Composers	2	Hector Berlioz	18
Renaissance Court and Church	4	Frédéric Chopin	19
Claudio Monteverdi	6	Robert Schumann	20
Music at the French Royal Court	7	Franz Liszt	21
Henry Purcell	8	Richard Wagner	22
Antonio Vivaldi	9	Giuseppe Verdi	23
Johann Sebastian Bach	10	Johannes Brahms	24
George Frideric Handel	11	Pyotr Ilyich Tchaikovsky	25
Christoph Willibald Gluck	12	Romantic Music in Russia	26
Josef Haydn	13	Nationalism in Central Europe	27
Wolfgang Amadeus Mozart	14	Gustav Mahler	28
Ludwig van Beethoven	15	Claude Debussy	29
Franz Schubert	16	Béla Bartók	30
Felix Mendelssohn	17	Igor Stravinsky	31
		Index	32

Throughout this book, you'll see QR codes like this one.
These are links to pieces of music on a tablet or smartphone.
You can find out more at the back of this book.
Don't worry if you haven't got a smartphone or tablet.
You can listen to the music at the Usborne Quicklinks
website, and you'll find links there to websites where you
can find out more about classical composers, too.

The First Composers

Composers are people who create music to play and sing.
Statues, pictures and instruments found in tombs show
that people have been doing this since ancient times.

In the Middle Ages, music was an important
part of religion. The modern way of writing
music down, called notation, began in
monasteries in Italy over 1,000 years ago.
It was developed by a monk,
Guido d'Arezzo.

Music was written by
hand in documents
called manuscripts.
They were often
beautifully illustrated,
like this one showing
notation for medieval
Italian music.

Guido d'Arezzo first lived
and worked at the Abbey of
Pomposa, near Ferrara, Italy.

Understanding old music

Before sound recording was invented about 120 years ago, the best
way to share music was to write it down. Now, experts learn about
early composers and their music by looking at old manuscripts.

One of the first
composers whose name
we know was Hildegard
of Bingen, a nun who
lived in Germany in the
11th century. She wrote
religious songs which are
still performed today.

This 19th-century model shows
Hildegard arriving at the Abbey
of Disibodenberg.

In the 12th century, Notre Dame Cathedral
attracted many musicians and composers.
This stained glass window comes from there.

Notation made music easier to
remember, so people were able to
sing two or more tunes at once.
This idea was called polyphony,
and Notre Dame in Paris was one
of the first places it developed.

The Renaissance

Starting in Italy in the 14th century, new ideas about learning and culture spread throughout Europe, in a period which became known as the Renaissance. As more people learned about music, singing and playing became popular pastimes.

The dome of Florence Cathedral, designed by Renaissance architect Brunelleschi, was finished in 1436.

Musicians painted around 1470 by Italian Renaissance artist Piero della Francesca

Renaissance ideas affected architecture, painting and music. These things became symbols of power for rich people and church authorities. Artists and composers moved around Europe to work at palaces and churches, taking their ideas with them.

Guillaume Dufay (1397–1474)

Italy attracted composers from all over Europe. Dufay was born near Brussels, but worked in several Italian and French cities. While working for Pope Eugene IV in Rome, he was asked to write a piece for the choir to sing at the opening of Florence Cathedral in 1436.

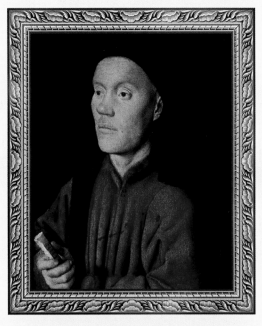

Some experts think this portrait, by Renaissance artist Van Eyck, is of Dufay. Both men worked at the Duke of Burgundy's court.

Josquin des Prez (1450-1521)

Josquin was one of the most widely known composers of his day. Born in northern France, he moved to Aix in southern France, then Milan, then Rome, where he sang in the Pope's choir. He wrote hundreds of pieces, mainly choral music and popular songs.

This printed version of Josquin's mass *L'homme armé* was made by Petrucci, an Italian pioneer of music printing.

After music printing was invented in the late 15th century, Josquin's pieces were among the first to be published.

Scan this code to listen to some music by Josquin.

Renaissance Court

During the Renaissance, many composers worked at the courts of kings, queens and aristocrats, making music for entertainment as well as church services. Some monarchs, including Henry VIII of England and his daughter Elizabeth I, drew composers from all over Europe.

Scan this code to listen to some music by William Byrd.

Thomas Tallis (1505-1585)

Tallis was a musician at the Chapel Royal for four English monarchs: Henry VIII, Edward VI, Mary I and Elizabeth I. *Spem in Alium*, his most famous piece, was composed for a choir of 40 singers. It may have been first performed in an octagonal tower at Nonsuch Palace in Surrey.

The ceiling of the Chapel Royal at Hampton Court, Henry VIII's palace

Nonsuch Palace, painted here by mapmaker John Speed, was said to be Henry VIII's grandest, most extravagant building project. But it was destroyed in the 17th century.

Spem in Alium was the first, and probably the only, choral piece ever written for 40 different voices, each singing a separate musical part.

William Byrd (c.1540-1623)

Byrd, who may have been one of Tallis's pupils, joined the choir of the Chapel Royal in 1572, working for Elizabeth I. As well as composing religious music and songs, he wrote pieces for stringed and keyboard instruments. Playing instruments became very popular during the Renaissance.

This painting shows Elizabeth I doing a dance called *la volta*. The musicians are playing stringed instruments called viols.

My Ladye Nevells Booke contains 42 of Byrd's keyboard pieces, written for a small keyboard instrument called a virginal.

Virginals were made of wood and often brightly painted. This one may have belonged to Elizabeth I.

... and Church

Apart from monarchs and aristocrats, the main employer of composers in the Renaissance was the Roman Catholic Church, based in Rome, Italy. Composers working there had to write music, teach the choir to sing, and play the organ and other instruments too.

Giovanni Pierluigi da Palestrina (c.1525-1594)

Palestrina was born near Rome, and as a boy sang in the choir at a large church, Santa Maria Maggiore. He published a book of religious music, which so impressed Pope Julius III that he gave him a job at St. Peter's, the greatest church in Rome.

Most of Palestrina's music was written for church choirs, but he also wrote non-religious songs called madrigals. He wrote some keyboard music too, which was probably played on the organ during church services.

The church authorities were very strict about what music was suitable for religious services. In this picture, Palestrina is showing his music to Pope Julius for approval.

Madrigals were written for small groups of singers, sometimes with instruments. Madrigal singing was a popular pastime.

Orlande de Lassus (c.1532-1594)

While Palestrina spent his life in Rome, other composers moved around. Born in Mons, now in Belgium, Lassus lived in many European cities. He had jobs at both churches and palaces, including the court of the Duke of Bavaria in Munich. He was one of the most famous musicians of his day, and taught many other composers.

Lassus wrote nearly 60 masses and hundreds of other religious pieces. His non-religious songs used words from five different European languages.

This painting by Hans Mielich shows Lassus conducting musicians at the Bavarian court.

Claudio Monteverdi (1567–1643)

In Italy at the end of the 16th century, art and architecture began to change, and so did music. The new style, often more dramatic and elaborate than Renaissance art, is usually known as Baroque. New instruments were invented, which composers used to accompany a few solo singers or players. This led to new types of music, both for voices and instruments.

Born in Cremona, northern Italy, a town famous for making stringed instruments, Monteverdi joined the court of Mantua in 1590. At first, he wrote church music and madrigals in a Renaissance style, but soon he began to experiment.

Claudio Monteverdi, painted by Bernardo Strozzi in about 1630

In 1607, Monteverdi wrote the first famous opera – a play in which actors sing instead of speak. It was called *L'Orfeo* and it was composed for the Duke of Mantua. Opera soon became popular all over Europe.

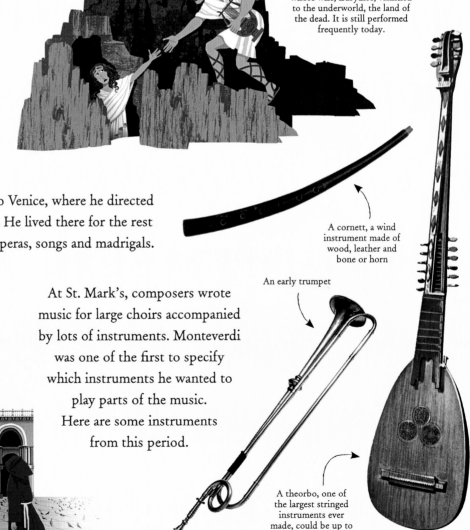

L'Orfeo tells the story of Orpheus, a musician from a Greek myth, whose wife, Eurydice, vanished to the underworld, the land of the dead. It is still performed frequently today.

Around 1613, Monteverdi moved to Venice, where he directed the music at St. Mark's Cathedral. He lived there for the rest of his life, writing church music, operas, songs and madrigals.

A cornett, a wind instrument made of wood, leather and bone or horn

An early trumpet

At St. Mark's, composers wrote music for large choirs accompanied by lots of instruments. Monteverdi was one of the first to specify which instruments he wanted to play parts of the music. Here are some instruments from this period.

A theorbo, one of the largest stringed instruments ever made, could be up to 2m (over 6ft) long.

Music at the French Royal Court

The French king Louis XIV lived in luxury at the Palace of Versailles, just outside Paris, but he spent a lot of money helping writers, architects, painters and musicians. He loved music and dance, often appearing as a dancer in ballets and plays. The king's ideas about music had a big influence on the composers he employed to write it.

Louis XIV's nickname, 'the Sun King', came from a costume he wore in a ballet composed by Lully in 1653.

Jean-Baptiste Lully (1632–1687)

Born in Florence to a family of millers, Lully learned music as a boy and moved to Paris to work for an aristocratic family. He attracted the attention of Louis XIV, who employed him to write ballets, operas, instrumental pieces and religious music, and as a conductor.

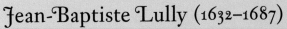

In those days conductors used a heavy stick to beat time. Lully died of a blood condition caused by hitting his foot accidentally during a concert.

Jean-Philippe Rameau (1683–1764)

After Louis XIV's death in 1715, the royal court had less influence over music, but composers like Rameau still had to rely on aristocrats and royalty for work. Born into a musical family in Burgundy, he settled in Paris in 1722 and became famous as a composer of operas. He also wrote a lot of instrumental music, particularly for the harpsichord, as well as books about music theory.

Characters from a 1908 performance of Rameau's first opera, *Hippolyte et Aricie*

French Baroque harpsichords were often very elaborate and decorated. Some, like this one, had two keyboards.

Scan this code to listen to some music by Lully.

Henry Purcell (1659–1695)

Purcell was born in England at a time of great political change. King Charles I had been executed in 1649, and for 10 years the country was ruled by a government that discouraged all forms of entertainment. Then, in 1660, the monarchy was restored under King Charles II, and music, plays and dancing became popular again. This period is often known as the Restoration.

Portrait of Purcell by Godfrey Kneller

Purcell was a musician for the Chapel Royal, a group of church officials and musicians in various royal palaces. By the age of 20, he was organist at Westminster Abbey, the most important musical job in England.

As organist, Purcell had to conduct the choir, play and write music too.

Scan this code to listen to some music by Purcell.

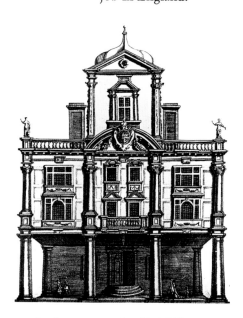

A 17th-century engraving of Duke's Theatre, London, where Purcell's *The Fairy Queen* was first performed in 1692.

Many new opera and playhouses opened at this time. Purcell wrote music for several operas and nearly 50 plays, often influenced by French and Italian Baroque music.

Purcell's most famous opera, *Dido and Aeneas*, is still often performed today. It tells the ancient Greek story of the Queen of Carthage during the Trojan Wars.

Aeneas takes leave of Dido, painted in 1630 by Reni Guido

Purcell composed many pieces for royal events. In 1694, he wrote the music for the funeral of Queen Mary II (see right). It was played again at his own funeral, the following year.

Mary II's funeral procession

Antonio Vivaldi (1678–1741)

Vivaldi was born in Venice and became one of the most famous composers of the Italian Baroque, a style which reached its peak in the first half of the 18th century. Instrument technology continued to develop at this time, making a wider range of sounds and notes available. Vivaldi took advantage of this, often creating dazzling combinations of instruments and trying out new ways of playing them.

Vivaldi learned the violin from his father, a barber who was also a musician. He taught music at an orphanage, and became a priest, nicknamed 'the red priest', probably because of his flaming red hair.

Some experts believe this is a portrait of Vivaldi, but it is not certain.

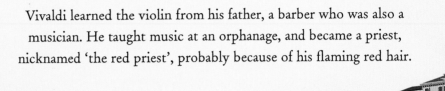

Vivaldi composed a huge amount of music, including over 500 concertos, many for the orphanage musicians. The most famous is *The Four Seasons*, a set of four violin concertos published in 1725.

In the 18th century, opera was one of the most popular forms of entertainment in Italy. Vivaldi wrote nearly 50 of them and organized performances in several cities, although his operas are rarely performed now.

This is from a modern performance of Vivaldi's opera *La Verità in Cimento*.

Part of the manuscript from Vivaldi's *La Notte*, a concerto for flute

In 1730, Vivaldi went to Vienna – possibly looking for a job with the Emperor Charles VI. But he was unsuccessful and died in poverty.

Vivaldi's music was forgotten after his death, and only rediscovered at the start of the 20th century. Italian conductor Arturo Toscanini (shown here) helped to make it famous again.

Johann Sebastian Bach (1685–1750)

Bach was born in Eisenach, Thuringia, central Germany, where his father was the director of the town musicians. Although never very famous during his lifetime, Bach is probably the best-known Baroque composer today. He wrote at least 1,200 pieces of music, and many of his children and grandchildren became musicians too.

As a boy, he was taught violin and harpsichord by his father, and clavichord by his brother. He worked at several churches in Thuringia, before becoming director of music at the court of the Duke of Weimar in 1708.

An 18th-century engraving of Weimar

A brilliant keyboard player, Bach often rewrote the instrumental music of other composers (including Vivaldi) so he could play it on the harpsichord or organ. So, although he never left Germany, he learned about the musical styles of other countries, such as Italy and France, and used them in his own music.

This harpsichord, made in Hamburg in around 1740, had several keyboards to enable different combinations of sounds.

In 1723, he became director of St. Thomas's music school, Leipzig, which provided music for the city's churches. He trained the musicians, conducted performances, and wrote music for religious services and city ceremonies.

St. Thomas's Church, Leipzig, where Bach worked for the last 27 years of his life

In 1747 Bach visited Emperor Frederick the Great at his palace in Potsdam. As a gift for the Emperor, he wrote *The Musical Offering*, a set of keyboard pieces full of puzzles, patterns and mathematical games.

1) The letters JSB

2) JSB mirrored

3) Together, 1 and 2 form a complex pattern

Bach designed this motif (or monogram) to sign his work. It's a pattern made from his initials.

Scan this code to listen to some music by Bach.

George Frideric Handel (1685–1759)

Handel, born in Halle, Germany, became one of the greatest Baroque composers. His father wanted him to be a lawyer, so he had to learn instruments in secret. But his playing was so impressive, his father was persuaded to let him study music. Unlike Bach, Handel left Germany as a young man and became rich and famous, mainly as a composer of operas.

First, in 1706, he moved to Italy, where he continued writing operas. Then, in 1710, Handel arrived in London, where he worked for many aristocratic and royal patrons, including Queen Anne, and Kings George I and George II.

Handel wrote some of his most famous music for royal celebrations. This painting shows a display of fireworks and illuminations on the River Thames in 1749, organized by George II. Handel wrote *Music for the Royal Fireworks* specially for the occasion.

By the 1730s, operas had become less fashionable, so Handel focused on oratorios instead. Oratorios are choral works that tell a story, but usually without costumes or acting, so were cheaper to perform.

Medal made to celebrate the coronation of King George II in 1727

This portrait shows Handel near the end of his life with a score of his most famous oratorio, *Messiah*.

Handel wrote music for the coronation of George II. One piece, *Zadok the Priest*, is played at every British coronation, and the anthem of the UEFA Champions League is based on it.

Christoph Willibald Gluck (1714–1787)

In the 18th century, a movement called the Enlightenment brought changes in philosophy, science and the arts. A rediscovery of the culture of ancient Greece and Rome influenced painters, writers and musicians. Composers such as Gluck began writing a simpler, smoother type of music, often known as the Classical style.

Gluck was born in Bavaria. After studying in Prague, he moved to Milan in 1737. His first opera, *Artaserse*, shown here, was performed in 1741 at the opening of the city's carnival.

The King's Theatre, London

He went to London in 1745 to be the composer at the King's Theatre. After moving around Europe, he settled in Paris, where some of his most famous operas were written. Later he moved to Vienna, which had become an important city for music.

This 18th century painting shows Gluck presenting his first opera to Queen Marie Antoinette of France.

Gluck wrote nearly 50 operas, some of which are still performed today. One of the most popular operas ever written is *Orfeo ed Euridice*, his version of the Greek myth of Orpheus (see page 6).

Gluck often used the same stories as Baroque operas, but in a more emotional way. With simpler songs and shorter instrumental pieces and dances, the effect was more dramatic and the story easier to understand.

One of the most famous singers of the time, Anna Milder-Hauptmann, appeared as Orpheus.

The title page of the first Italian edition of *Orfeo ed Euridice*

Josef Haydn (1732–1809)

Public concerts and dances grew in popularity in the 18th century, and more people learned to play instruments. Aristocrats set up permanent groups of musicians at their palaces, so composers like Haydn could write for orchestras and small groups. This helped the Classical style to take hold.

Portrait of Haydn at the piano, painted about 1790 by Austrian artist Johann Zitterer

Born in Rohrau in Austria, Haydn was a choirboy in Vienna, then worked there as a musician. In 1761 he began working for the Esterházys, an aristocratic family with palaces in Austria and Hungary.

Musicians playing in the concert room in the Esterházy palace at Fertod in Hungary

The Esterházys altered Haydn's contract so that he was able to work for other people too. He made two long, successful visits to London, and finally settled in Vienna.

Haydn is known as 'the father of the string quartet'. He wrote about 70 quartets and 104 symphonies, and his musical ideas influenced composers for hundreds of years.

This is the front page of a set of keyboard pieces Haydn wrote for two pupils, the Auenbrugger sisters.

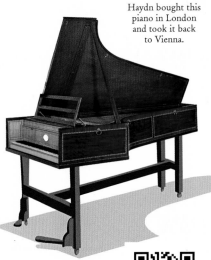

Haydn bought this piano in London and took it back to Vienna.

The Farewell Symphony – a hint for a Prince

In 1772, Prince Nikolaus stayed with the Esterházys a long time, but his musicians wanted to return to their families in Eisenstadt. So Haydn wrote a symphony in which the players leave the stage one by one at the end. When the Prince heard it, he allowed his musicians to return home.

Scan this code to listen to some music by Haydn.

Wolfgang Amadeus Mozart (1756–1791)

Mozart is one of the most famous composers of all time, and his music was celebrated all over Europe. But fame didn't bring him wealth or independence. He always had to rely on rich patrons for work.

Mozart's father Leopold was a violinist and composer at the court of the Prince of Salzburg in Austria. Mozart learned keyboard and violin as a young child, and wrote his first pieces when he was only five years old.

The Mozart family performing in Paris, painted in 1777 by French artist Louis Carmontelle

Mozart's sister, Maria Anna, was also a gifted musician. Realizing his children's talent, Leopold took them on long tours of Europe to perform in public and for aristocrats.

This map shows the extent of Mozart's journeys. Travel was long, uncomfortable and often dangerous. But it made him very famous.

Later Mozart worked as a court musician in Salzburg until he lost his job in 1781. He moved to Vienna, where he met many important musicians, including Haydn. Although his music became very popular, he was often in debt.

By the time he died at the age of 35, Mozart had composed more than 40 symphonies, 20 string quartets and 20 operas, as well as songs, religious music, piano music and nearly 60 concertos. Weeks before his death, he conducted the first performance of *The Magic Flute*, one of his most famous operas.

Costume designs for a 19th-century production of *The Magic Flute*

Mozart died before this portrait by Austrian painter Josef Lange could be completed.

Ludwig van Beethoven (1770–1827)

The transition from the 18th to the 19th century was a time of great political change in Europe. Beethoven's life reflected this. He was the first composer who was able to make a living from music without needing to work for wealthy employers.

A miniature portrait of Beethoven as a young man

Beethoven was born in Bonn, Germany. As a child he learned piano, violin and composition from his father and others. In 1787, he visited Vienna briefly and met Mozart. Later he went to live there, studying with Haydn.

Vienna had many public concert halls. One of the most famous was in a park called the Augarten, shown here.

In 1795 he gave his first concert in Vienna, playing a piano concerto he had composed. It impressed many aristocrats who gave him money to help his career. His first published pieces appeared that year, and were very successful. Soon he was famous all over Europe.

Beethoven made money by playing at concerts and selling his music to publishers. He had rich patrons, but never let them control his work. His music was often bold and adventurous. He wrote nine symphonies, a violin concerto, five piano concertos, 32 piano sonatas, 16 string quartets, an opera, songs and religious music.

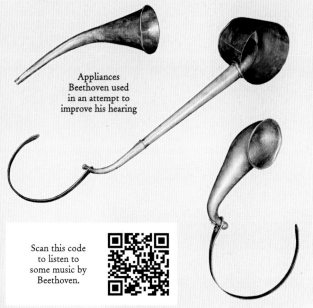

Appliances Beethoven used in an attempt to improve his hearing

In 1796 Beethoven started to have hearing problems. By 1814 he was completely deaf and stopped performing. But he continued composing right up to the end of his life. When he died, as many as 20,000 people may have attended his funeral.

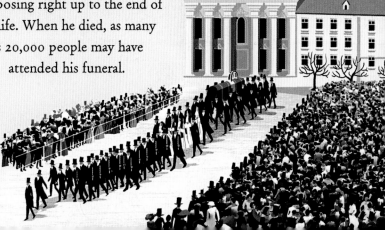

Scan this code to listen to some music by Beethoven.

Franz Schubert (1797-1828)

Born in Vienna, Schubert was part of a group of writers and artists who often met to share ideas. He played his music for friends at events called Schubertiads. By the time he died at the age of 31, Schubert had written over 600 songs, nine symphonies, chamber music and over 100 piano pieces.

Schubert performing at one of his Schubertiads

A portrait of Schubert painted by Gábor Melegh, a Hungarian artist

Schubert was very short-sighted. This is a pair of his glasses that have survived.

Towards the end of his life, Schubert lived at his brother's apartment in Vienna. This is now a museum.

For the songs, Schubert used poems by many 19th-century poets, including Heinrich Heine. Some of them are very dramatic, based on supernatural subjects. Others are beautiful love songs.

Illustration for *Loreley*, a poem by Heine that Schubert set to music.

Romanticism

In the 19th century, many writers and artists explored the idea that the world was ruled by feelings and unexplained forces. This was known as Romanticism, and it affected composers too including Schubert and Mendelssohn.

One of the first Romantic artists, Caspar David Friedrich painted highly atmospheric scenes like this one, called *The Dreamer*.

Scan this code to listen to some music by Schubert.

Felix Mendelssohn (1809-1847)

Mendelssohn was born in Hamburg, Germany and began writing music as a child. One of his most famous pieces was based on Shakespeare's play *A Midsummer Night's Dream*. He composed it when he was only 17.

A portrait of Mendelssohn aged 12, by German Romantic artist Carl Begas

A scene from *A Midsummer Night's Dream* painted by English Romantic artist William Blake

Mendelssohn visited many parts of Europe, including England, where he met Queen Victoria.

Mendelssohn wrote piano pieces, songs, and orchestral and chamber music. He also toured Europe as a conductor, and was one of the first to use a baton.

He kept diaries of his travels, and sent letters and sketches to his sister, Fanny, herself a pianist and composer.

Baton used by Mendelssohn when he conducted at Birmingham Town Hall in 1846

A link with the past

By the 19th century, Baroque composers such as Bach and Handel had been forgotten. But these composers are well known today, partly because Mendelssohn helped make their music popular again by conducting it in concerts.

While living in Leipzig, Germany, Mendelssohn sketched the church where Bach had lived and worked 100 years earlier.

A drawing of Fanny Mendelssohn by the artist Wilhelm Hensel, who became her husband

Hector Berlioz (1803–1869)

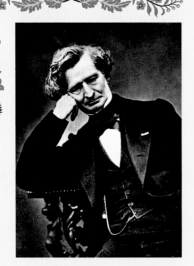

Berlioz was one of the first composers ever to be photographed.

Berlioz and Chopin both studied at the Paris Conservatoire, shown here in the 1830s.

Berlioz was a true Romantic who lived an adventurous, passionate life. His route to success as a composer was unusual. He didn't start music lessons until he was 12 and his parents were not enthusiastic about him being a musician.

Berlioz was born near Grenoble in France, and went to Paris in 1821 to train as a doctor. But he hated it and began studying music instead. He soon became well-known as a composer and conductor.

In 1827 Berlioz saw two Shakespeare plays in Paris and became obsessed with one of the actors, Harriet Smithson. To describe his feelings, he wrote the *Symphonie Fantastique*, one of the first pieces to tell a story in music without words. Berlioz wrote a booklet to be read at performances, which outlined the plot.

In 1832, Berlioz invited Smithson to a concert where he conducted the symphony. She realized the piece was about her, and the couple married the following year.

Events in the story include a glamorous ballroom where dancers whirl around to a waltz...

...an evening in the countryside where he hears shepherds playing pipes...

...a nightmare where he dreams he has murdered Harriet and is executed for the crime...

...and a witches' dance.

This caricature of Berlioz made in 1846, shows him conducting a huge orchestra, including a cannon, before a terrified audience.

Berlioz wrote less music than other composers, but some of his pieces are long and require huge numbers of players and singers. Over 400 musicians took part in the first performance of his *Grande Messe des Morts* in 1837. Some people were said to have fainted because the music was so loud.

Frédéric Chopin (1810–1849)

During his lifetime, Chopin was equally well known as a pianist and composer. Most of his compositions were written for the piano and he performed many of them himself at concerts. With his expressive, emotional music, he was one of the first celebrity performers of the Romantic period.

A silhouette of Chopin by the artist Georg Philipp

Born near Warsaw, Poland, Chopin learned music as a child, and later studied piano and composition at the conservatory in Warsaw. He gave his first concerts in Warsaw and Vienna, and published his first pieces, in the 1820s.

In 1831, the Russian army invaded Warsaw. Chopin moved to Paris, where he became part of a group of pianists that also included Liszt (see page 21).

The Paris pianists: Chopin is standing in the middle, Liszt is sitting on the right

Chopin became hugely famous as a pianist, even though he only gave about 30 public concerts in France. He preferred to play for friends in his apartment.

In 1836 Chopin met George Sand, a French author. Some of his most famous pieces were written at her house at Nohant in central France. Many famous artists and writers visited them there.

This hand-painted fan owned by George Sand shows scenes of her life at Nohant, including Chopin.

Chopin wrote hundreds of piano pieces, some influenced by traditional Polish dances such as the polonaise and mazurka. Others, called nocturnes, are very atmospheric and have beautiful song-like melodies.

Scan this code to listen to some music by Chopin.

Robert Schumann (1810-1856)

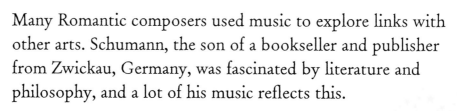

Many Romantic composers used music to explore links with other arts. Schumann, the son of a bookseller and publisher from Zwickau, Germany, was fascinated by literature and philosophy, and a lot of his music reflects this.

Scan this code to listen to some music by Schumann.

A 19th-century silhouette of Schumann in middle age

Schumann began by studying law, following his family's wishes, although he had learned the piano as a boy, and began composing and writing about music. However, in 1830, he heard the famous violinist Paganini play, and was so impressed by the experience that he returned to music.

Paganini was the most famous musician of his day. His playing was so dazzling that some people thought he had magical powers.

At first, he hoped to be a concert pianist, but after injuring his hand he concentrated on composing. He wrote hundreds of piano pieces, songs, chamber music and symphonies – many linked to literature.

Schumann's injury may have been caused by a chiroplast, a device some 19th-century pianists used to strengthen their hands.

One of Schumann's most famous sets of piano pieces is *Papillons*, meaning 'butterflies' in French. He based them on a description of people at a masked ball in a novel by German writer Jean Paul.

In 1834, Schumann started a music magazine which is still published today. It praised the music of Chopin, Mendelssohn and Brahms, as well as earlier composers.

NEUE ZEITSCHRIFT FÜR musik
5 september oktober 2006
DAS MAGAZIN FÜR NEUE TÖNE
Global Ear I Afrika

The magazine Schumann started is one of the longest-running music publications in the world.

Schumann suffered on and off from bouts of mental illness. After his death, his wife Clara Wieck, a celebrated concert pianist, continued to perform and promote his music, preparing much of it for publication.

Carved profiles of Robert and Clara Schumann

Franz Liszt (1811–1886)

Piano music was very popular in the 19th century and some pianists became huge celebrities. The most famous of all was Liszt, who toured Europe for years playing to massive, enthusiastic crowds.

Liszt was born in Doborján, Hungary, and he learned the piano from his father. He gave his first concerts at the age of 9. Wealthy patrons were so impressed they offered to pay for his musical education in Vienna.

A portrait of Liszt as a young boy

This silhouette by the artist Bithorn shows Liszt conducting.

At the age of 16 he moved from Vienna to Paris, where he met Berlioz and Chopin (see pages 18 and 19). Hearing Paganini play in 1832 inspired him to become a virtuoso pianist.

Liszt was soon performing all over Europe. Audiences often screamed, fainted and fought to get close to him.

As well as playing and conducting, Liszt composed a lot of music – including some of the most difficult piano music ever written – intended to display his skills as a pianist. He wrote songs, orchestral music and religious pieces too.

Liszt composed 13 symphonic poems – orchestral pieces that tell a story or describe a scene. Some were inspired by poetry, legends and paintings.

A 19th-century cartoon of Liszt performing

In the 1860s, after disappointments and sadness in his personal life, he joined a monastery near Rome and stopped performing. But he began again towards the end of his life.

One of Liszt's symphonic poems, *Hamlet*, is based on Shakespeare's play.

Liszt became so famous his image was used in advertising. This advertisement for chocolate shows him as an old man, dressed as a priest.

Chocolat Suchard

Franz Liszt.

Richard Wagner (1813–1883)

Wagner at the age of 30

Born in the same year, Wagner and Verdi (see opposite) were the two most important opera composers of the Romantic period. Opera became hugely popular in the 19th century, though it developed differently in each European country. In Germany, Wagner devised a revolutionary way of combining words, drama and orchestral composition.

Wagner was born in Leipzig, Germany. He learned the piano as a child, but wanted to be an author. He wrote his first play when he was 13, but decided to turn it into an opera and began studying composition.

In the 1830s, Leipzig was famous for its enormous fair, shown here.

Wagner wrote songs, piano pieces and orchestral music, but is best known for his operas. Unlike most other composers, he wrote the words too, often basing the tales on ancient German legends. The most famous, *The Ring*, is a group of four operas, and lasts a ground-breaking 20 hours.

The Ring takes place by the River Rhine. It tells the story of an enchanted ring, an evil dragon, magical beings, fires and battles.

Wagner had an opera house built at Bayreuth, Germany, where his operas were performed at a festival every year. After his death, it was run by his wife Cosima (Liszt's daughter), and by other family members. The festival continues today.

The opera house at Bayreuth, being built in the 1870s

This painting shows (from left to right) Cosima, Wagner, Liszt and an unknown figure.

Giuseppe Verdi (1813–1901)

Verdi was the most famous Italian composer of his time, and composed some of the best-known operas ever written. When he was young, Italy was made up of many small states and Verdi became part of a political movement to join them into a single country. For some, his music represented the spirit of Italian nationalism.

This 19th-century advertisement for stock shows Verdi and his birthplace.

Verdi was born near Busseto, Italy. He was a paid church organist by the age of eight, and started writing music a few years later. In 1830 he went to study in Milan, and soon began working at La Scala, Italy's most famous opera house. His first opera, *Oberto*, was performed there in 1839.

In 1842 his opera *Nabucco* was a huge success. Over the next ten years it was performed all over Europe, and in New York and Buenos Aires. Verdi was one of the first composers to receive worldwide recognition during his own lifetime.

Nabucco is a biblical story about a Babylonian king, Nebuchadnezzar II.

Verdi composed some songs and religious music, but mainly he wrote operas. These are based on a variety of subjects – ancient history, modern love stories and political dramas. One of the most famous, *Aida*, is a tragedy set in Ancient Egypt.

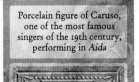

Porcelain figure of Caruso, one of the most famous singers of the 19th century, performing in *Aida*

Verdi was paid a massive amount of money to write *Aida*. It was composed for the opera house in Cairo, which was built to celebrate the opening of the Suez Canal in 1869. This special 3-D photograph shows a scene from an early performance.

Falstaff, Verdi's final opera, is based on Shakespeare's comedy *The Merry Wives of Windsor*. After the première in 1893, the applause lasted for an hour.

Johannes Brahms (1833–1897)

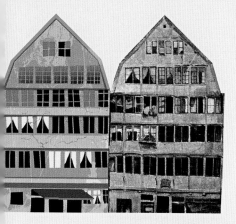

Although a lot of Romantic composers drew inspiration from other arts, others continued to write music that wasn't 'about' anything except music itself. Brahms took musical ideas from 18th century composers, such as Bach, Mozart and Beethoven, and reworked them in a 19th-century Romantic style.

The building in Hamburg, where Brahms lived as a child, was destroyed during the Second World War.

Born to a poor family in Hamburg, Germany, as a young man Brahms made money by playing the piano in dance halls and taverns. In these places he heard a lot of traditional melodies, some of which he later adapted in his own compositions.

At the age of 20 he toured Europe as a pianist. He met many composers, including Liszt, and the violinist Joseph Joachim, who introduced him to Robert and Clara Schumann. They encouraged him as a composer.

Joseph Joachim and Clara Schumann, painted by a German artist named Menzel

In 1854, Clara was the first person to perform Brahms's music in public, and she championed his career. They remained lifelong friends.

Brahms wrote symphonies, concertos, chamber music, songs, piano pieces and religious music. Some of his music is very difficult to play, but he also wrote simpler pieces for amateur music makers.

Brahms was one of the first musicians to be recorded. In 1889, an engineer named Theo Wangemann visited him in Vienna and recorded him playing one of his piano pieces.

Wangemann worked for Thomas Edison, the American inventor of sound recording.

A tinted black and white photograph of Brahms

Pyotr Ilyich Tchaikovsky (1840–1893)

Tchaikovsky was the best-known Russian composer of the 19th century, and the first to become internationally famous. His ballet music is some of the most popular ever written and he developed new ways of writing for orchestra that made his music dazzling and exciting.

Tchaikovsky as a young man, painted by Russian artist Yury Lehman

Tchaikovsky studied law in St. Petersburg, destined for a career as a civil servant. In 1862, he enrolled at the music conservatory, and showed such talent he was soon offered a job as professor at the Moscow Conservatory.

The St. Petersburg Conservatory opened in 1862. Tchaikovsky was one of the first students.

His music was first performed in public in 1865, and his first symphony three years later. But teaching left him little time to compose and the pay was poor. In 1877 he started to receive financial support from Nadezhda von Meck, a wealthy admirer of his music. He was able to give up his job and become a full-time composer.

Tchaikovsky wrote operas, symphonies, concertos, songs, chamber music and music for several ballets, including *Swan Lake*, *Sleeping Beauty* and *The Nutcracker*.

Stage design for the first performance of *The Nutcracker*

Scan this code to listen to some music by Tchaikovsky.

Romantic Music in Russia

In the 1850s, many Russian artists felt their culture was too dominated by the traditions of western Europe. A group of composers in St. Petersburg aimed to create a new Russian style of music, drawing on Russian stories, paintings and folk songs.

Night on Bald Mountain depicts a scene from a Russian play about witches

Mussorgsky in Russian army uniform

Modest Mussorgsky (1839–1881)

was born near St. Petersburg. He studied the piano and wrote music as a child. He was a soldier, then a civil servant, but continued to study music and compose. In 1867, he wrote the first version of one of his best-known pieces, *Night on Bald Mountain.*

In 1873 he wrote *Pictures at an Exhibition*, a set of piano pieces based on paintings by his friend Viktor Hartmann, who had recently died. The pieces are linked by a theme representing someone walking around an art gallery.

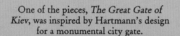

One of the pieces, *The Great Gate of Kiev*, was inspired by Hartmann's design for a monumental city gate.

Nikolai Rimsky-Korsakov (1844–1908)

was born near St. Petersburg and played the piano and composed as a child. He was an officer in the Russian navy for many years, but taught music and composed at the same time.

His most famous piece is *Scheherazade*, written in 1888, based on the *Arabian Nights* stories. One of his last pieces, *The Golden Cockerel*, is an opera based on a story by Russian writer Alexander Pushkin.

Stage design for an early production in Paris of *The Golden Cockerel*

Scheherazade was used for a famous ballet. In the first production, the principal dancer Nijinsky wore this costume, designed by Leon Bakst.

Nationalism in Central Europe

Scan this code to listen to some music by Dvořák.

The spirit of national pride that affected Russia was also felt in other parts of Europe. In Bohemia (then part of the Austrian empire, now the Czech Republic), composers began to create a national musical style using features of the country's traditional songs and dances.

Bedrich Smetana (1824–1884)

was born in Litomsyl, east of Prague. He learned music as a child, then went to Prague to study. After hearing Liszt play there, he decided to become a professional musician. At first he made a living by teaching, conducting and playing the piano.

In 1866 he finished *The Bartered Bride*, his most famous opera. In it, Smetana adapted Czech songs and dances. It was not an instant success, but after he revised it in 1870 it was soon performed all over Europe.

Smetana playing the piano for friends

Unlike the operas of Wagner and Verdi, *The Bartered Bride* told the story of ordinary people in a Czech village.

Antonin Dvořák (1841–1904)

was born near Prague and played the violin and piano as a child. He worked as a pianist, teacher and conductor, but in his early 30s he decided to concentrate on composition. In 1874, he won an important prize for composers. Brahms was one of the judges and helped him with his career.

Many of Dvořák's pieces include rhythms and tunes from traditional Czech music.

Dvořák was soon internationally famous and in much demand. He visited Britain eight times, and in 1892 went to New York to be head of the music conservatory. There he listened to a lot of African-American music, which influenced his best-known symphony, *From the New World*.

Dvořák with his family and friends in New York.

Dvořák was awarded a doctorate by the University of Cambridge in 1891.

Gustav Mahler (1860–1911)

Mahler as a young man

Like many of the arts, music began to change towards the end of the 19th century. Composers such as Mahler explored complicated concepts: the subconscious, national identity and religion. As a result, they often used more complex harmonies and wrote more ambitious pieces.

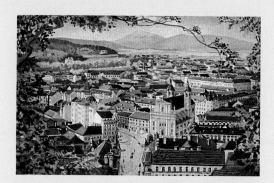

Mahler conducted more than 50 operas in the Slovenian town of Ljubljana.

Mahler was born in Kaliste, a small town in Bohemia. He began playing the piano as a child and went to the Vienna Conservatory at the age of 15. Five years later he composed his first orchestral piece, and got his first job as a conductor.

Mahler had little time to compose. Many of his pieces were written during summer holidays. He had several 'composing huts', like this one next to a lake in Austria.

During his lifetime, Mahler was best known as a conductor. He held important jobs in Prague, Leipzig, Budapest, Hamburg, Vienna, and other European cities, and worked in London and New York too. But pressure of work often made him ill and unhappy.

From 1897 to 1907, Mahler was conductor-in-chief at the Vienna Opera House, one of the most prestigious musical jobs in Europe.

Mahler's Eighth Symphony is one of the most ambitious pieces ever written, requiring a huge orchestra, eight solo singers, two choirs and a children's choir. Over 3,000 people attended the first performance in Munich in 1910.

The Eighth Symphony is often known as the 'Symphony of a Thousand', although Mahler himself did not give it this name.

Claude Debussy (1862–1918)

As the 20th century approached, Debussy and other composers began experimenting with new harmonies and scales – looking for new ways to use and combine instruments. Audiences were often startled by the results.

Born near Paris, Debussy entered the Paris Conservatory at the age of 10. In 1884 he won a composition prize and studied in Rome for two years. After returning to France he worked mainly as a teacher and conductor.

Debussy with his beloved daughter Claude-Emma, known as Chou-chou

In 1889, a percussion orchestra called a gamelan, from Java, Indonesia, performed at a huge trade and cultural exhibition held in Paris. Debussy was fascinated by the sounds it made, and this affected his music.

Most Europeans had never heard music from Asia before.

The Eiffel Tower was built for the 1889 World's Fair in Paris.

SOUVENIR DE L'EXPOSITION UNIVERSELLE DE 1889
LA TOUR EIFFEL

Debussy was involved with a group of painters and writers known as the Symbolists, who often explored myths and the subconscious in their work. Debussy based one of his best-known orchestral pieces, *Prélude à l'après-midi d'un faune*, on a poem by Stéphane Mallarmé, a Symbolist poet.

Mallarmé's poem was turned into a ballet, shown here, by Russian dancer Nijinsky. It was first performed in 1894.

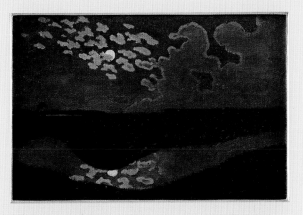

This picture, *Clair de Lune* (meaning 'moonlight') by Félix Vallotton, was painted around the same time as Debussy wrote *Clair de Lune*.

Debussy once told a pupil to imagine that the piano had no hammers. *Clair de Lune* is slow, quiet and still, suggesting moonlight on water. It is like a painting in sound.

Scan this code to listen to some music by Debussy.

Béla Bartók (1881–1945)

Music changed rapidly in the 20th century for many reasons. The development of sound recording meant that music could be easily captured, shared and broadcast. People were able to travel and discover new sounds. Wars and political upheavals disrupted people's lives. Bartók's life reflected all these changes.

Bartók as a young man

Born near Szeged in Hungary, he played the piano by the age of four and wrote his first music when he was nine. From 1899 to 1903, he attended the Music Academy in Budapest.

Bartók was very interested in traditional music. He visited many parts of Europe to record and write down folk songs and dances.

In 1911, he wrote the opera *Bluebeard's Castle*, based on a French story about a prince who murders his wife. It was first performed in 1918 at the end of the First World War.

A Hungarian postage stamp commemorating Bartók and *Bluebeard's Castle*

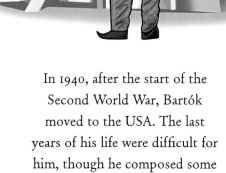

The Miraculous Mandarin, one of Bartók's best known pieces, is a ballet based on a violent, shocking story. It was banned after its first performance in Germany in 1926.

To the left and right are costume designs by Enrico Prampolini for a production of *The Miraculous Mandarin*.

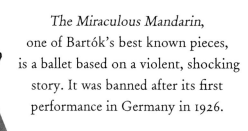

In 1940, after the start of the Second World War, Bartók moved to the USA. The last years of his life were difficult for him, though he composed some of his best music there.

A cartoon of Bartók, announcing a concert he gave in New York

Bartók wrote orchestral pieces, songs, string quartets and a lot of piano music, including *Mikrokosmos*, a series of 153 piano pieces. These are simple to start with, but get slowly more difficult.

Igor Stravinsky (1882–1971)

Many artists, writers and composers left Europe for the USA in the Second World War. Some found it difficult to settle, but Stravinsky lived and worked there successfully until he died. Like composers centuries before him, he took musical traditions from one country to another.

Scan this code to listen to some music by Stravinsky.

A drawing of Stravinsky by Picasso (1920)

Tamara Platnovna Karsavina dancing in the first performance of *The Firebird*

Born near St. Petersburg, Stravinsky learned the piano as a young boy, and studied composition with Rimsky-Korsakov. In 1909, his music was heard by Diaghilev, a producer planning performances of Russian ballets in Paris.

When *The Rite of Spring* was first performed in Paris, audiences were so shocked that they rioted.

Diaghilev asked Stravinsky to write music for a new ballet, *The Firebird*. When it was first performed in Paris in 1910, it made Stravinsky an instant star. He wrote two more ballets for Diaghilev – *Petrushka* and *The Rite of Spring*.

The Rake's Progress is based on paintings by 18th-century English artist William Hogarth.

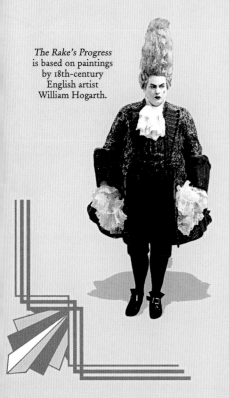

Stravinsky conducting, during a visit to Moscow

In 1951 he wrote one of his most famous operas, *The Rake's Progress*. The words are by British poet W. H. Auden, who Stravinsky met in Hollywood.

Stravinsky moved to the USA in 1939. He settled in Hollywood, close to many European writers and painters. As well as working as a conductor and teacher, he continued to compose.

Stravinsky became so famous in Hollywood that he was awarded a star on the Hollywood Walk of Fame.

Index

A
aristocrats, 4, 5, 7, 13, 14, 15
Austria, 13, 14

B
Bach, Johann Sebastian, 10, 17, 24
ballets, 7, 25, 29, 30, 31
Baroque, 6, 8, 9, 10, 12, 17
Bartók, Béla, 30
Beethoven, Ludwig van, 15, 24
Belgium, 3, 5
Berlioz, Hector, 18, 21
Bingen, Hildegard of, 2
Bohemia, 27, 28
Brahms, Johannes, 20, 24, 27
Brussels, 3
Budapest, 28, 30
Byrd, William, 4

C
cathedrals, 2, 3, 6
chamber music, 16, 17, 20, 24, 25
Chapel Royal, 4, 8
choirs, 3, 4, 5, 6, 8, 28
Chopin, Frédéric, 19, 20, 21
choral music, 3, 4, 5, 11
church music, 4, 5, 6, 10
Classical style, 12, 13
concertos, 9, 14, 15, 24, 25
concerts, 13, 14, 17, 19, 21
conductors, 9, 17, 28, 29, 31

D
D'Arezzo, Guido, 2
Debussy, Claude, 29
de Prez, Josquin, 3
Diaghilev, 31
Dufay, Guillaume, 3
Dvořák, Antonin, 27

E
England, 4, 8, 17, 27
Enlightenment, the, 12

F
Florence, 3, 7
France, 2, 3, 10, 12, 18, 19, 29
funerals, 8, 15

G
Germany, 2, 5, 10, 11, 15, 17, 20, 22, 24, 30
Gluck, Christoph, Willibald, 12

H
Handel, George Frideric, 11, 17
harpsichords, 7, 10
Haydn, Josef, 13, 15
Hungary, 13, 21, 28, 30

I
Italy, 2, 3, 5, 6, 7, 9, 10, 23

K
keyboards, music for, 4, 5, 7, 10 see also piano music

L
Lassus, Orlande de, 5
legends, 21, 22
Liszt, Franz, 19, 21, 22, 24, 27
London, 8, 11, 12, 13, 28
Louis XIV, 7
Lully, Jean-Baptiste, 7

M
madrigals, 5, 6
Mahler, Gustav, 28
manuscripts, 2
masses, 5
mazurkas, 19
Mendelssohn, Fanny, 17
Mendelssohn, Felix, 16, 17, 20

Middle Ages, 2
Milan, 3, 12
monarchs, 4, 5, 7, 8, 9, 10, 11, 17
monasteries, 2, 21
Monteverdi, Claudio, 6
Mozart, Wolfgang Amadeus, 14, 15, 24
Mussorgsky, Modest, 26

N
New York, 23, 27, 28, 30
Nijinksy, 26, 29
nocturnes, 19
notation, 2

O
operas, 6, 8, 11, 12, 14, 15, 22, 23, 25, 26, 27, 31
oratorios, 11

P
Paganini, 20, 21
palaces, 3, 4, 5, 7, 8, 13
Palestrina, Giovanni Pierluigi da, 5
Paris, 2, 7, 12, 18, 19, 21, 29
piano music, 14, 15, 16, 17, 19, 20, 21, 22, 24, 26, 30
Poland, 19
polonaises, 19
polyphony, 2
popes, 3, 5
Prague, 12, 27, 28
printing, 3
Purcell, Henry, 8

R
Rameau, Jean-Philippe, 7
religious music, 2, 4, 5, 6, 7, 15, 21, 23, 24
Renaissance, the, 3, 4, 5, 6
Restoration, the, 8
Rimsky-Korsakov, Nikolai, 26, 31

Romanticism, 16, 18, 19, 22, 24, 26
Rome, 3, 5, 21, 29
Russia, 25, 26, 27

S
Schubert, Franz, 16
Schumann, Clara, 20, 24
Schumann, Robert, 20, 24
Shakespeare, William, 17, 18, 21, 23
Smetana, Bedrich, 27
sonatas, 15
songs, 3, 4, 5, 6, 12, 14, 15, 16, 20, 21, 22, 23, 24, 25, 26, 30
sound recording, 2, 24
Stravinsky, Igor, 31
string instruments, 4, 6
string quartets, 13, 14, 15, 30
Symbolists, the, 29
symphonic poems, 21
symphonies, 13, 14, 15, 16, 20, 24, 25, 28

T
Tallis, Thomas, 4
Tchaikovsky, Pyotr Ilyich, 25
traditional music, 24, 26, 27, 30, 31

U
USA, 27, 28, 30, 31

V
Venice, 6, 9
Verdi, Giuseppe, 22, 23
Vienna, 9, 12, 13, 14, 15, 16, 19, 24, 28
violinists, 20, 21, 24
Vivaldi, Antonio, 9, 10

W
Wagner, Richard, 22
Warsaw, 19
Westminster Abbey, 8